The Shakespeares

The Shakespeares

Nathaniel Harris

ILLUSTRATED BY KEN KIRKLAND

J M DENT & SONS LTD

First published 1976

Text © Nathaniel Harris, 1976
Illustrations © J. M. Dent & Sons Ltd, 1976

Printed and bound in Great Britain by
Morrison & Gibb Ltd., London and Edinburgh
for J. M. Dent & Sons Ltd
Aldine House · Albemarle Street · London

This book is set in Baskerville 11 on 12 point.

ISBN 0 460 06676 5

Contents

Illustrations

Settling in Stratford

A Sunday in September 1568. The town councillors of Stratford-upon-Avon move down the High Street in procession, on their way to the Church of the Holy Trinity. With them are their wives, rather stiff in their best gowns. And in front of the procession, carrying the corporation maces and kicking and cuffing away stray animals and children, march the town's sergeants in their buff-coloured leather jerkins.

The leading group of councillors are the aldermen, in black gowns trimmed with fur; and at their head is John Shakespeare, the new high bailiff—or, as we should say, the mayor of Stratford. As bailiff, John is much more than the town's First Citizen for a year. He is chief executive, chief magistrate, and agent of the central government far away—a hundred and forty-odd kilometres away—in London. He is a real power in his small world, and has earned the respect which greets him and his wife as they enter the church and take their places in the front pew.

This must be a great moment in Shakespeare's life: the climax of twenty years' work for himself and for the town. Powerful and respected, with an established business, a wife and two children (and another on the way), he may look back on his boyhood in the countryside and congratulate himself on the good luck that brought him to Stratford.

The idea of this book is to trace John Shakespeare's progress from country boy to bailiff, to look at the way he and his family lived, and to discover what happened to them later on.

John came from Snitterfield, a little village about five kilometres north of Stratford. His father, Richard Shakespeare, was a yeoman—not, in other words, a gentleman with his own coat of arms, but a solid, respectable farmer. The accuracy of the description was proved when Richard died in 1561, leaving goods valued at £38.17s.—by no means a fortune, but a tidy sum all the same.

Richard's son John must have known Stratford well. It was only an hour's walk from Snitterfield, and the Shakespeares would have brought their produce into the town to sell on market days. So it was perfectly natural for John to become apprenticed to a trade there, some time in the 1540s; his brother Henry followed in their father's

Town councillors in procession

footsteps and farmed around Snitterfield for the rest of his life.

John's apprenticeship would have lasted seven years, as was customary in most 'mysteries' (crafts) including John's—that of Glovers, Whittawers and Collarmakers. We first hear of John as a glover in 1556, but he was probably in business on his own account in 1552, when he was fined twelve pence for creating a dunghill in Henley Street, where he lived. Incidentally, the offence didn't blight his career; in fact, in an age careless of hygiene it was the equivalent of getting a parking ticket.

Once set up in Henley Street, John Shakespeare could get married. Perhaps it had all been arranged long before, since he must have known the girl for years. She was Mary Arden, daughter of Robert Arden, who owned the Snitterfield property farmed by Richard Shakespeare. The Ardens lived at Wilmcote, five or six kilometres to the west of both Snitterfield and Stratford, in a big, well-built farmhouse complete with barns, byres and a great stone dovecote capable of holding hundreds of birds. The match was a fine one for John Shakespeare. The Ardens of Wilmcote were related to the Ardens of Park Hall, near the little town of Birmingham; and these Ardens were one of England's great families, with a history stretching back beyond the Norman Conquest. True, the Wilmcote Ardens were a very minor branch of the family, and Mary was the youngest of *eight* daughters (possibly something of a glut on the local marriage market). But all the same, Mary's freedom to marry 'beneath her' was a peculiar feature of English life that is worth noticing.

Classes mattered in sixteenth century England: they behaved differently, demanded and received different treatment, looked up to or down to one another. But the boundaries were never impossible to cross. In Spain a gentleman would starve rather than soil his hands by trading, and a girl of gentle birth would have to enter a convent if she had no dowry to attract a man of her own class. In England class was mainly fixed by how much money a man had and how he was prepared to spend it: if you dressed, behaved and spent like a gentleman, you *were* a gentleman. In the middle ranks of society adjustments were going on all the time. A gentleman's children could marry a yeoman's without any feeling of shame; and the yeoman himself could aspire to gentility.

In this instance there were solid material benefits for the aspiring yeoman. Mary married John Shakespeare shortly after her father's death in 1556, bringing with her a portion of £6.13s.4d. and substantial properties at Wilmcote. Within the year, John had begun his civic career and Mary had become pregnant. They were already settled citizens of Stratford.

An apprentice glover

The town

By modern standards Stratford was hardly more than a village—a huddle of a few hundred low dwellings, half-hidden among masses of elm trees. Even within the county of Warwickshire it ranked in importance below Coventry, a great centre of the cloth-making industry, and was rivalled by Warwick and Kenilworth, towns whose nearby castles belonged to the magnificent Dudley brothers, earls of Warwick and Leicester, who basked in the favour of Queen Elizabeth.

But Stratford was a respectable enough size by the standards of the time. Only a handful of English towns were substantially bigger, and even the biggest had no more than twenty thousand inhabitants. The one exception was London, already huge out of all proportion, with a population of several hundred thousand. For the rest, there were only a few dozen towns about the size of Stratford; the majority of the English people did not live in towns at all, but in thousands of small settlements—like Snitterfield and Wilmcote—scattered over the land.

In a land of villages and hamlets a town like Stratford took on an extra importance as a local centre. In fact it was really a kind of extension of the countryside, providing a market for farm produce, a range of craft services from ironwork to shoemaking, and a variety of shop goods from hose to tobacco and ale. Men and goods flowed in and out of the town from the surrounding countryside. A country-man might turn craftsman and stay, like John Shakespeare; equally, a successful tradesman would buy land and farm it.

Nor was there any physical separation between town and country. The tight rows of shops in the two main streets had big gardens behind them, and in the rest of the town there was plenty of space and greenery—gardens, orchards, even brooks running between the houses, supporting a population of birds and small animals as well as domestic livestock. And in this little town the countryside proper could be reached from any point by a walk lasting ten minutes at the very most.

Everything would have been sweetness and light—but for the stinking slops and scraps and piles of dung, and the fat, noisy presence of pigs. The public cleaning service consisted of a widow who was paid 6s.8d. a year to sweep the market place, and an old man who cleaned up the bridge. The rest of Stratford was supposed to be kept in decent order by the householders: each was to clean out the gutters and ditches in front of his home, and all rubbish was to be taken to one of the dumps on the edge of town. This was not much to ask in such a small place: John Shakespeare, for example, had only to go to the far end of Henley Street. But few people cared enough to make the effort, including the civic-minded John, whose dunghill was not his last breach of council regulations: within a few years he was fined fourpence for not clearing out his gutter. Later we shall find the same lack of sanitation—and the same mixture of sweet and sour smells—inside the home.

But first we can explore the actual streets and buildings of sixteenth century Stratford; one advantage of its smallness is that we can get to know it fairly thoroughly.

The town lies on the west bank of the river Avon, which flows past it in a roughly south-westerly direction. The road to Banbury, Oxford and London lies across the river—across the many-arched fifteenth century stone bridge built by Sir Hugh Clopton, a Stratford mercer who made good in London, became lord mayor, and used part of his wealth to improve and beautify his native town.

Suppose we cross Clopton bridge from the other direction, as visitors to the town. The bridge goes on to become a stone causeway, and this gives way to Bridge Street, which would be a good wide thoroughfare if it were not split in two by a line of shops and stalls down the middle ('Middle Row'). We pass the inns competing for our custom—the Bear and the Crown on our left, the Swan on the right—and get to the end of Bridge Street, which is effectively the town centre.

From here roads lead off in several directions. In front of us is a fork. To the right is Henley Street, where the Shakespeares live, leading out of Stratford towards Wilmcote, and eventually on to the town of Henley-in-Arden. The left fork is Wood Street, going on to Greenhill Street, a rather run-down part of the town.

Sharp left from Bridge Street is Stratford's main street, running roughly parallel with the river and changing its name (High Street - Chapel Street - Church Street - Old Town) as it winds down to the Church of the Holy Trinity, some way beyond the built-up area close to the river. At the junction of Bridge Street and the High Street stands the Market Cross, a sort of large shed raised on timber columns. This is the centre of Stratford's chief market, held every Thursday, and of the twice-yearly fair. Here too are the stocks, the pillory and the whipping post, where drunks, prostitutes and thieves provided a warning example—and, such being the tastes of the time,

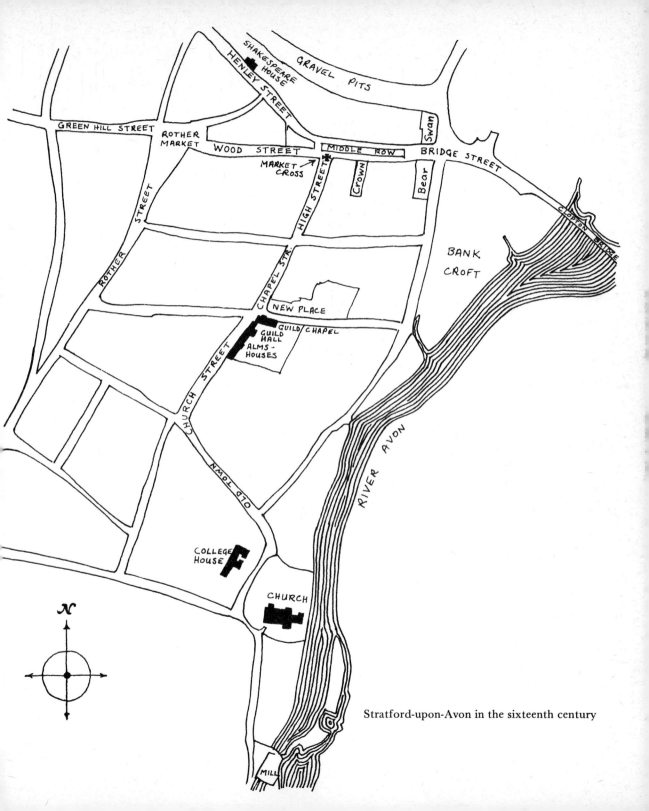

Stratford-upon-Avon in the sixteenth century

Market Cross

public entertainment. (Brutal, humiliating punishments were easier and cheaper than keeping people locked up, though various buildings were used as a gaol, including 'the Cage', a big shop on the corner of the High Street.)

Immediately below the Market Cross, in the High Street, are the biggest shops, selling everything from American tobacco to knitted stockings bought up in bulk at Evesham by Adrian Quiney the mercer. Further down the road are the big private houses. Above all there is New Place, the nearest thing in Stratford to a palace, standing on the corner of Chapel Street and Chapel Lane. New Place had been built in the 1490s by Sir Hugh Clopton, and was the outward sign of his enormous success in life. In John Shakespeare's day it is still an impressive sight, though in a bad state of repair: a three-storey, sixty-metre wide brick and timber house, set back from the road behind a courtyard and complete with barns, gardens and orchards.

Directly opposite New Place, still on the main road, are the Guild buildings: the Guild chapel, the Guild hall where the town council meet, and almshouses for Stratford's aged and homeless poor. Then, as 'Old Town', the road runs down to the pleasant parish church, most of its stones—and its wooden spire—dating from the thirteenth and fourteenth centuries. Opposite the church is the College House, another fine big building; and a little further on, by the river, a mill stands as the last outpost of the town.

The rest of sixteenth century Stratford can be described in a few words. Parallel with the High Street on the side away from the river is Rother Street, wide enough to contain the cattle and hide markets ('rother' is an old word for an ox). Parallel with Bridge Street and Wood Street run two sets of lanes. These streets form a simple two-by-three grid containing most places of note within the town. There are also the corporation-owned gravel pits at the back of Henley Street; and just below the bridge, beside the river, is a wedge of common called Bank Croft, on which Stratford people can graze their horses, sheep, cattle and swine for an hour a day. Beyond that, there is only the friendly, familiar countryside. So much, then, for our tour of Stratford (and for the present tense).

Over the centuries the pattern of life changed very little in this small community, though individuals and families prospered and failed, flourished and died out. But in John Shakespeare's time there was one set of events that deeply affected the whole town. This was the religious revolution—the 'Reformation'. In the uncertain years around the middle of the sixteenth century, England swung backwards and forwards between the new Protestant and the old Catholic faith. The conflict was only decided in 1558, when Queen Elizabeth came to the throne and established what proved to be a lasting, moderately Protestant Church of England.

The effects were felt over a period of years. Teachers and priests attached to the Old Faith lingered for a while, often trying to come to terms with the new, before going to ground or emigrating. Catholic families were hard-hit—and sometimes ruined—by regular fines for non-attendance at church. But more was involved than a change in personnel in the religious and social hierarchy. Protestants favoured a plainer, simpler form of worship; they despised Catholic cults, rituals and church decorations as 'superstition', and wanted to drastically reduce the power of the priesthood. In practical terms—in Stratford terms—this meant transforming both the church and the government of the town.

Down to 1547 the Church of the Holy Trinity was a collegiate church—that is, run by a 'college' of half-a-dozen priests. Their main job was to say masses for the soul of John of Stratford, his friends, and the kings and queens of England; John, a fourteenth century Archbishop of Canterbury, had financed the college for that purpose, and had converted a chapel in Holy Trinity into a chantry where priests could say the masses. An Act of 1549, passed in the reign of the Protestant king Edward VI, dissolved all such chantrys and put an end to two hundred years of masses said for John of Stratford. Holy Trinity became a plain parish church; the College building passed into private hands and rivalled New Place for the title of Stratford's finest residence; and the chantry priests were presumably pensioned off.

The transfer of property from the church and its allies was a vital aspect of the English Reformation: it undermined the old and financed the rise of new institutions. For this reason the Reformation was a social as well as a religious revolution, and can be said to mark the end of the Middle Ages. In Stratford this was signalized by the dissolution of the Guild of the Holy Cross. The Guild was a typical medieval institution—a religious association which was also a mutual benefit society, club and charity. With the help of wealthy donors it had maintained the impressive group of buildings opposite New Place—the Guild hall, the fine grey Chapel (largely rebuilt by the ubiquitous Sir Hugh Clopton), and the almshouses—as well as becoming landlord of many of Stratford's most valuable properties. The Guild had a large part in running the town's affairs, but soon after its abolition Stratford received a proper charter, setting up a town council and making it independent and self-governing. The

18

council paid its expenses (and the salaries of the vicar and schoolmaster) out of the income from the Guild's property, most of which it took over. It even met in the old Guild hall and repaired to the Guild Chapel to hear prayers.

The new borough of Stratford came into existence in 1553—just as John Shakespeare was beginning his rise to prominence in Henley Street.

Early years in Henley Street

In 1556 John Shakespeare bought two houses, one in Greenhill Street and the other in Henley Street. Presumably this Henley Street house was not the one he already occupied, but the one next door; for we find him a few years later living in two Henley Street houses which had been converted into one.

This double house was a typical Stratford building of the kind that is often miscalled 'Tudor' though there are many medieval examples. It is known as 'half-timbered' because its skeleton was made of wooden beams, the areas between being filled, in with rubble, or a mixture of twigs and clay ('wattle and daub'), boarded and plastered over ('lath and plaster'); this gives the style its distinctive brown/black-and-white appearance. It was a natural and economical method of building in any district rich in trees and poor in stone—like Stratford. The steep gabled roof of the Henley Street house had long chimney-stacks to carry sparks well clear of it, and dormer windows that jutted out above the pitch of the roof. Glass was becoming common in windows, replacing horn and other, even less efficient substances; but it was still expensive enough to keep the window area small, and instead of large sheets of glass there would be a diamond-patterned grid of lead—'a lattice' into which small pieces of glass could be fitted. In other words, though 'picturesque', the half-timbered house was severely practical, shaped by the materials and technology available at the time.

Inside, John Shakespeare's house was dim when no fire was lit, and the stone floor helped to make it rather chilly except in high

Section of a half-timbered house

summer. Downstairs, where John had his workshop and Mary her kitchen and living room, the raftered ceiling was low; the upper storey was also cramped, though the steep angle of the roof gave an illusion of greater spaciousness.

The furnishings would have been substantial rather than decorative, and rather sparse by our standards. An exception would be the large number of cloth hangings painted with leafy designs or religious tags, adding colour to the interior and acting as draught-excluders. Everything in sight would have had the slight irregularity that comes from being hand-made, especially when the objects in question are for use rather than ornament. Furniture, painted hangings, embroideries, iron implements, pottery cups and bowls, kitchenware of brass, pewter and lead—all would have lacked the precise machine edges, the flawlessly smooth surfaces and the exactly matching hooks, knobs, ears, lips and bases that we are used to. On the other hand they would have a kind of sturdy individuality—and they would be made to last. There were no power drills or electric saws: wood had to be cut and chiselled and joined by hand. Similarly, keys and locks, grates and fire irons, hinges and hasps, had to be heated and beaten into shape by the local blacksmith. Too much effort and expense was involved in making household goods to treat them lightly or put up with gimcrack jobs. Apart from the very rich, who might be influenced by changes in fashion and style, a man expected his possessions to be taken over and used by his children after his death, and perhaps even by his children's children. Almost all Elizabethan wills, for example, give precise directions as to the disposition of household effects.

Furniture was particularly massy: slab-like tables with feet held together by 'stretchers', long rectangular chests that could double as seats, wide squat sideboards and cupboards, perhaps with some fancy decorations carved by a carpenter neighbour. John and Mary probably had wooden chairs with arms, but not many: perhaps one each, and one for a distinguished visitor. Children and servants almost certainly made do with stools. There would probably be a settle too—a bench with a high back and wings to exclude draughts. (The elaborate measures taken against draughts do not inspire confidence in the efficiency of Elizabethan plasterwork and heating.)

The austerity of all this hard, straight, wooden furniture must have been softened by the presence of embroidered cushions, covers and other stuffs. Such luxuries made the Elizabethan home a rather more comfortable and friendly place than its fifteenth century counterpart. One writer of the 1570s has left us an interesting account of such changes. William Harrison, an Essex clergyman, noted in his

21

Description of England that three things had been 'marvellously altered' within a few years. One change was the widespread installation of chimneys, replacing the old open fires whose fumes passed through a hole in the roof—after blackening the room and thickening the atmosphere. Another was the replacement of wooden platters and spoons by pewter, tin or silver ware. And finally there was the development of sleeping luxury with the increasing use of feather beds and pillows. Harrison, with a parson's concern for moral fibre, was inclined to think that Englishmen were worse off for abandoning a straw pallet, single rough sheet and good round log under the head, though it is hard to believe that he himself followed the old ways. Of course the people who were experiencing the new luxuries were the middling people like the Shakespeares, not the poor; and no doubt John and Mary were the only people in the house who slept in anything we should regard as comfort.

In sanitation and hygiene there was no advance at all. The Queen's godson, Sir John Harrington, was soon to invent a type of water closet or lavatory, but although Elizabeth installed one at Richmond the idea never caught on, even among the aristocracy. Ordinary people like the Shakespeares were satisfied by the use of a bucket in one of the nooks in the house. Baths were taken—once in a rather long while—in a tub in front of the fire, or in the form of a dip in a nearby pond. The house itself must have been appallingly unhealthy, with a carpet of rushes, only rarely swept out and replaced, into which all kinds of rubbish and scraps were carelessly tossed. The Elizabethans evidently believed that if they killed the smell of filth they also destroyed the danger of infection. One antidote to smells was to scatter sweet herbs among the rushes. Even better results were obtained by putting the herbs into a bed-warmer—a round metal container with small perforations, attached to a long pole. When heated, the herbs gave off a delightful aroma, and a child or servant could carry this 'plague pan' through the house, rapidly 'disinfecting' it—without, of course, altering the fact that the floor was a breeding-ground for disease.

With its low ceilings, small windows, space-consuming hangings and large population, the Shakespeare house—and thousands of houses like it in England—must have been a claustrophobic place. Fortunately the children could spend most of their days outdoors, for there was no high-speed traffic in the town, and the fields were only minutes away.

Inside, privacy was almost impossible. Partitions were rudimentary, and since there were no corridors, anyone who wanted to reach the furthest bedroom would have to pass through all the others. (Even the architects of the rich had not thought of putting in corridors, but their clients were able to get some privacy by pulling the curtains shut round their great four-poster beds.) To us, a place like the Shakespeares' home would have seemed a rabbit warren, inhabited by a master who worked at home, a mistress constantly busy with household matters and cooking, perhaps a servant girl and/or an apprentice, and a rapidly increasing band of small children.

As there were no reliable methods of contraception, most married women who were not sterile became pregnant at regular intervals. Mary Shakespeare was not exceptionally fertile, but she bore eight children who were baptized. (She may well have had some unrecorded miscarriages too.) The compensating factor in these times, preventing a disastrous population explosion, was the high death-rate. The expectation of life was much lower than it is now, and childbirth and childhood were full of dangers: of Mary's eight children only five grew to maturity and only one reached old age.

The first seven arrived with fair regularity, about once every two or three years. Joan, born in 1558, died sometime within the next few years. The next child, Margaret, died five months after her birth in November 1562. But then two healthy boys followed: William in April 1564, Gilbert in October 1566. A second Joan followed in 1569 (her name tells us that the earlier must have been dead by this date), and then came Anne in 1571 and Richard in 1574. With three boys in the family, the Shakespeare name was reasonably certain to survive, and John and Mary presumably did what they could to make sure there were no more children; with Mary around forty—old for motherhood in those times—the possibility must have seemed remote.

Working days

Work was right at the centre of home life. The family was a much more self-contained group than it is now, whether it lived by farming in the country or by craft work in a town. In many instances mutual aid must have been more important than ties of affection in holding the family together. Mary would have woven her own wool, and she and John probably brewed their own ale. Like many of their neighbours they kept stores of malt and corn, and several barrels of beer. The garden would have provided them with some vegetables, and they may have had one or two animals which the children could graze on Bank Croft. We can see that, even in the town, houses were not very far removed from farms.

As mistress of the Henley Street house, Mary Shakespeare would have worked hard to keep a household of at least seven people clothed, fed, cleaned and heated; and it is doubtful whether the efforts of a servant girl compensated for the absence of sewing and washing machines, cookers and vacuum cleaners.

Mary's domain was the kitchen. Cooking was done in the great hearth, within which large fire irons framed a big fire. The food was roasted on a spit over the fire, or stewed in large cauldrons hanging from an iron bar. Preparing, cooking and serving the food, and cleaning up afterwards without detergents, must have been almost a full-time job in itself.

Meals would have been unsophisticated but abundant. The Elizabethan breakfast, at six or seven in the morning, generally involved quantities of porridge, with perhaps some ale to set the workers up for the day. Now and later there was fresh bread, baked in the wall-oven by the hearth and probably variable in quality; it was shovelled in and out of the oven on a long, flat wooden object like an oar.

The whole family would be present at the main meal, which was midday dinner; the boys would come home from school for it, and, if they were well-raised children, would help their sisters to lay the table. Soon it would be groaning under quantities of meat, for this was what Englishmen loved best of all, astonishing foreigners by the quantities they consumed. Beef, mutton and veal were their staples, with pork, poultry and rabbit, pies, puddings, sausages and bacon; and for hard winters there were pickled meats such as brawn and souse (pickled pork). Dairy foods, fruit and nuts were also popular, but vegetables were regarded without enthusiasm as make-weights. Most people liked artichokes best, but filled up on cabbages, peas and beans. They were probably grown in the garden behind the Shakespeare's house, along with cucumbers, turnips, carrots and radishes. We notice the absence from this list of tomatoes and potatoes— natives of the Americas that were known only as exotic upper-class luxuries. On the other hand imported foodstuffs such as onions, olives and oranges reached Stratford from time to time.

Then there were the days on which it was compulsory to eat fish:

A family dinner

A typical provincial family

twice a week and during Lent. Many people disliked the prohibition as a left-over of 'popery' (Friday is still fish-day for Catholics), though the government's motive was actually to ensure the prosperity of the fishing industry, which provided England's sailors in time of war. And it was no great hardship to observe the regulation, for even far from the sea England's streams and ponds were thronged with fish.

The Shakespeares' dinner would have been served on plate (probably pewter) and consumed with the aid of a knife. Forks—the latest subtle Italianate innovation—were hardly known yet in London, let alone Stratford.

With the meal went beer, ale or wine—the latter probably Sack (Spanish or Canary) or the interestingly named Bastard, the *vin ordinaire* of the time. A long boot-like leather jug might still be used for drinking beer (held over the shoulder, Spanish peasant style). But even modestly prosperous provincials would now be able to afford another luxury popularized by the Italians—drinking glasses.

Everybody looked forward to the sweet things: 'sugar meats' such as marchpane (marzipan), all sorts of biscuits and tarts, and comfits, suckets and sweetmeats preserved under thick layers of sugar paste. The Englishman had a terribly sweet tooth—until it was eaten away by sugar—and the Shakespeares were probably no exception.

Looking after the family's clothes was another difficult job for the housewife. Naturally the extravagant London fashions would not have been followed in Stratford. Fine cambric shirts, doublets slashed to show lavish stuffs inside them, ultra-rigid 'peascod belly' bodices and tent-like farthingale skirts were crushingly expensive and utterly impractical for a busy craftsman and his wife. But even the modest ruffs worn by sensible provincials—male and female—must have made a housewife's existence a misery, for they had to be cleaned and then ironed into pleats and starched to stand up stiff and proud. Apart from his ruff, John probably wore a sturdy, hard-wearing doublet, at first made of a rough material such as kersey, and later, as he became better off, something finer—but never anything as extravagant as the London beau's velvets and silks. His hose, shoes and gown would have been equally conservative, though we may suppose that his gloves were particularly splendid, if only as a form of advertisement. Mary may well have stuck for a long time to the simple style of her first youth, with a bodice and skirt beneath a long gown; but eventually she must have succumbed to the long-lasting vogue of the farthingale, at least to the extent of padding her hips with a circular wad of cloth, converting her skirt into a roll farthingale or 'bum roll'. Later still, perhaps, both John and Mary may have dressed more grandly for formal civic occasions; but they can never have looked anything like the gorgeous courtiers whose portraits can so easily mislead us about sixteenth century dress.

Mary's contribution was important, but John Shakespeare's workshop was the vital centre of the household, since the whole future of the family depended on it. As a glover and whittawer, John made gloves from sheep and goat skins and tawed, or dressed, the softer, white skins such as deer and kid. He was not allowed to cure or work with cowhide or pigskins because they were the province of the tanners. It was the guild's business to enforce such demarcations, protecting their members by keeping out interlopers and sharing out jobs so that there was work for as many as possible. As we have seen, John Shakespeare himself must have served a seven-year apprenticeship before becoming a journeyman or a fully-fledged master with his own workshop.

Guild regulations would come to seem oppressive as trade expanded, calling for more competition and new initiatives. But although there was a surge forward in industry and trade during the sixteenth century, the Elizabethan world was still one of limited resources, output and markets; and in such a world guild restrictions were an insurance against starvation in bad times.

Even so there were seven or eight glovers in Stratford alone. Gloves were high fashion, it is true, perfumed and decorated—even jewelled—and worn on hats as ladies' favours as well as on the hands. All the same, it is surprising that the town could support so many people engaged in the same trade. Though the local gentry may have patronized John Shakespeare and his fellow craftsmen, much of the Stratford glovers' business must have consisted of orders for standard everyday gloves at fourpence a pair, and for accessories such as belts, jerkins, aprons and purses. John must have been hoping to attract pretty ordinary customers when he laid out his wares in the 'penthouse' of Henley Street—the shed-like porch built on to the front of the left-hand house. And when he set up his stall near the Market Cross every Thursday, he must have seen mainly familiar faces, those of customers keen to secure bargains rather than pay out for luxury goods. It was probably only twice a year, at the fairs, that fancy workmanship was much in demand. Then even the husbandmen who usually had nothing to spare—even the apprentices and yokels, lucky if they had any cash at all—might want something special for themselves or their sweethearts.

For the rest of the time, John's daylight hours would be spent downstairs in his workshop, using his dividers to measure and his

John Shakespeare's house and shop

paring knife to cut out patterns from the skins—the trank (top and palm of the hand) all in one piece including the fingers: the thumb separately, and for each hand six little fourchettes, the sidepieces used to join the fingers. Then, if there was no fancy work to be done, the various pieces could be sewn together with a special gloving needle and some strong thread. Years of practice and experience—knowing how much a given material would stretch and comparing hands—would simplify most tasks, though a good deal of hard labour remained.

At the end of the working day, at five or six o'clock, the family would have a light meal: supper. When John had become one of Stratford's leading citizens he would do his civic duty and hang a lantern outside the house (this was Stratford's nearest approach to street lighting). And Mary probably put out the dole-cupboard, filled with stale bread and scraps to placate passing vagrants. By nine o'clock, like other respectable people, they had put out the lantern and gone to bed.

So John Shakespeare worked and prospered. Like any sensible man he spread his risks, buying more houses, farming land outside the town, dealing in wool, and doubtless selling off his stores of malt and corn when they were in short supply and the price was high. He was becoming one of Stratford's most substantial citizens, and as such could be expected to play a great part in the town's affairs.

The rise of John Shakespeare

From the time its charter of incorporation was granted in 1553, Stratford was a borough or corporation ruled by a town council—a bailiff, fourteen aldermen and fourteen burgesses. The council was self-selecting: gaps in the ranks were filled by nominees of the council, and each year the aldermen selected one of their number as bailiff, more or less by rotation. In practice this meant that the wealthier citizens had a monopoly of power in the town, since they chose new members only from people of their own sort. What is more, this situation would have met with general approval: according to Elizabethan thinking, common folk were too ignorant even to know their own interests, and it was only right and proper that those with 'a stake in the country' should rule. This can hardly be called anti-democratic since the very assumptions of democracy—of some sort of equality between human beings—were lacking. The power of rich over poor and of 'gentle' over common—like the power of men over women and parents over children—was looked on as part of the natural order.

John was accepted into the Stratford élite as a burgess at about the time of his marriage. In 1557 he was given his first responsible position as one of the borough's two tasters of ale and bread. The job did not call for a connoisseur, but for a conscientious inspector who would make sure that the regulations about quality, weight and price had been obeyed. Elizabethan local authorities had multitudinous functions of this sort, representing the kind of close control over every community that the Privy Council in London would have liked to see. Strict parental authority, with no room for personal initiative, was the ideal of sixteenth century governments, though they lacked the communications, personnel and money to enforce it—except in a haphazard way. Local government was no more successful in many instances, but quality control was probably effective in a small community: where consumers knew one another and gossip travelled fast, traders could not afford to be caught adulterating their goods.

The following year John was promoted to constable—one of the four whose job it was to lead the watch round Stratford at night, calling the hours and keeping a sharp eye open for intruders, drunks and incipient fires. The occasional drunk was a minor nuisance, but the threat of fire to tight rows of wooden houses was real; while serious crimes were most likely to be committed by intruders—especially the thousands of vagabonds, beggars, old soldiers and swindlers roaming the country.

Among his other functions a constable signed the minutes of each court session. John Shakespeare scratched on to the page a symbol of his trade—the special dividers he used. This may have been a professional flourish, and similar 'sign-manuals' were certainly used by literate craftsmen—but not all the time. And as there is not even one signature or set of initials by John Shakespeare, he probably did not know how to form them. This was hardly surprising in a country-bred boy, since schools were essentially town institutions.

If John really was illiterate, the fact was no hindrance to his career. In 1559 he became affeeror, which meant it was his responsibility to decide the fines to be paid for certain minor offences. Two years later he was appointed chamberlain. He had to look after the corporation's money, make payments to plague victims, the destitute, and occasional entertainers, note expenses for feasting local worthies, and present a regular set of accounts. He was so successful that he was kept in office for four years—a very great compliment. The element of accountancy involved suggests that John may have been able to write after all, but the job could probably have been managed by a dynamic supervisor with a strong memory and a quick way with tallies, the notched wooden sticks that had been used for doing sums since the Middle Ages. Towards the end of John's tenure of office, in 1563-4, the plague struck hard at Stratford. John's baby son William survived unscathed, but it looks as though Margaret—and perhaps also the first Joan—were carried off. John himself was noticeably generous at this time in his donations towards poor relief.

In 1565 John Shakespeare took a long step forward: he became an alderman, one of the élite-within-the-élite at Stratford. He replaced William Bott, a financier from Coventry who had bought the Clopton's house, New Place. Bott was an aggressive, quarrelsome type, and had let fly with some indiscreet remarks about the council in the course of prosecuting a poor painter, accused of stealing timber from Bott's garden. According to Bott there had never been such a thing as an honest man on the council (except himself, presumably); and when the council sent for him to explain his behaviour he was equally insulting. Understandably, the council decided that he should be 'expulsed', and elected John Shakespeare to replace him.

As an alderman, John wore the fur-trimmed gown and a special ring, and was addressed as 'Master Shakespeare'. Perhaps more important for an ambitious man, he was now eligible to become high bailiff of Stratford.

He had not long to wait, which confirms that he was genuinely popular and able. In September 1568 he was elected bailiff, with a neighbour, alderman Wheeler, as his deputy (High Alderman). We have seen that some impressive ceremonial trappings went with the bailiff's office. Before every public occasion the senior sergeant called for him, and the two sergeants escorted him and his deputy to council meetings at the Guild hall, to inspect the markets and fairs, and on the formal Rogation Day tour of the parish boundaries. In church and chapel too, John and Mary Shakespeare would automatically be given the place of honour.

Ceremony aside, the bailiff of Stratford presided over meetings of the council (which took place on average once a month), and

Constables patrolling the town at night

exercised the powers of a justice of the peace within the town boundaries. (The regular J.P.s were members of the gentry whose powers went far beyond dispensing justice.) Once a month during his term of office John Shakespeare heard cases involving small sums of money—mainly actions for the recovery of debts—at the court of record. And twice a year he held a court-leet to make new police regulations and judge breaches of the old ones.

As head of the council John had to look after its properties in the town; negotiate with the Earl of Warwick, still theoretically lord of the manor with some claims on Stratford; witness and confirm leases, indentures of apprenticeship and similar documents; administer poor relief and properly maintain the almshouses; act as coroner, investigating the circumstances in which townspeople died; supervise the conduct of the market and the use made of the common land, the bowling alleys and the archery butts; fix beer and bread prices every Thursday night, after the market; enforce the laws against extravagance in dress (especially the statute laying down plain woollen caps as the proper headgear for Sundays); investigate non-attendance at church; and even punish cases of flagrant immorality.

Described in this way, the bailiff of Stratford sounds like a bureaucrat in some totalitarian state, interfering with people's lives at every turn; and that is what the Privy Council would have liked him to be. But in practice the bailiff and his assistants had neither the resources nor the wish to control people closely: fines, for example, were hard to collect, and debts seem to have remained unpaid for years at a time, despite the judgements of the court of record. John Shakespeare himself was always sueing or being sued about something or other, without much in the way of visible results; and we sometimes get the impression that litigation was more of a rural hobby than a serious attempt to have justice done.

The formal titles and official proceedings should not make us forget that we are looking at a small group of people, most of whom would have known one another. Familiarity must have rubbed away some of the solemnity of interviews between aldermen and other townsmen, and many decisions must have been influenced by local knowledge and personal sympathies. Behind the records there must be a good many unwritten stories—perhaps of a popular man let off because he has had some bad luck; of an unpopular one penalized on the slightest excuse; of the town drunk tolerated for behaviour worse than that of a rowdy apprentice, who would have to be discouraged from setting other young men an undesirable example. In other words there must have been plenty of give and take, including some audible jokes and half-stifled laughs at the expense of any council member who became too pompous.

Many of the council's activities were directed towards preserving peace and the social order. This was particularly important in England, where there were dangerous religious tensions, where the army was small and local policing rudimentary, and where even in good times the poorest section of the population only just managed to survive. If taverns were allowed to sell drinks to artificers during working hours, there would be brawling, damage to property, loss of working time; so it was forbidden. If journeymen and apprentices were allowed out at night they were likely to cause trouble that the watch could not handle; so they were ordered to be home by nine o'clock. And if a poor girl became pregnant without marrying, she and her baby would have to be supported out of the parish funds; so a serious attempt was made to discover the father and make him wed or pay. In fact the close regulation of Elizabethan life—and of medieval life before it—was, paradoxically, a way of coping with the problems of a weak central authority and a poor society.

Often the central government—the Privy Council—took a hand in maintaining peace and order. In times of dearth, for example, the corporation might be told to investigate the citizens' holdings of corn and malt. Those with large holdings would have to release them (instead of hoarding them till the price soared), and the order would go out that less barley was to be used for malting. The object was not only to protect the poor but also to prevent discontent building up into rioting and rebellion. But this kind of government action usually met with only limited success, since its execution depended on the co-operation of the wealthier people who were councillors and justices of the peace—the very people with an interest in hoarding and selling at high prices.

The most important orders sent out from London to the provinces concerned politics and religion—which in that age were virtually one and the same. For example, attendance at church at least once a month was required as a demonstration of political loyalty. The Queen herself had said that she had no wish to 'make a window into men's souls': if they would attend church no one would question them any further to discover how far they were still attached to the old Catholic faith. Those who would not conform to this extent were under suspicion: they might be sufficiently fanatical to want to overthrow the 'heretic' Elizabeth and put her Catholic cousin, Mary Queen of Scots, on the throne. Many Catholics were in fact loyal enough subjects, but it must have seemed a sound policy to weaken their influence by making them poorer, quite apart from the fact that

Investigating corn stocks

heavy and regular fines for non-attendance were a useful source of government revenue and an encouragement to the less resolute to conform.

As it happened, John Shakespeare's year in office was a quiet one, though towards its end, in the summer of 1569, the Privy Council ordered regular searches to be made for vagrants—not just beggars, but any person of no known fixed abode. Illegal gatherings were to be put down, and archery—the traditional form of local self-defence—was to be encouraged. But the real alarums and excursions started soon after Shakespeare's successor had been installed. Rumours of rebellion began to take on credibility as the Warwick-shire gentry organized a body of troops ready to march north; Stratford contributed towards the preparations. And in fact the Earls of Northumberland and Westmorland did try to raise the North for the 'Old Faith' in November 1569, entering Durham and defiantly celebrating mass in the cathedral. Mary, Queen of Scots, who had been a prisoner in England for the past year, was hastily moved south from Leicestershire; for a time she was held at Coventry, only a short distance from Stratford. And the Earl of Warwick and his army—including Warwickshire levies—marched north. In the event the rebellion collapsed almost at once, but it served to show the instability of the new order. And for a moment it brought the little town of Stratford into touch with the great world, where heads rolled and battles decided the fate of dynasties.

The Northern rebellion had repercussions in Stratford. There and elsewhere it made it more uncomfortable to be a Catholic, especially if you held any kind of official position. That may be why Stratford's schoolmaster and vicar moved on, and was almost certainly why the curate, James Hilman, simply disappeared: he is down in the records as *fugitivus*, a runaway. The town council too was stirred into new activity. The Guild Chapel was already bereft of its ornately carved rood-loft and rood-screen, carvings and wall paintings; now the stained-glass windows were taken down and replaced by plain glass. Not long afterwards, in 1571, the current bailiff, Adrian Quiney, was authorized to sell off the copes and vestments in the possession of the authorities—sumptuous items of damask and velvet, loathed most of all by the increasingly vocal people who wanted a still more austere and radically Protestant Church of England. These 'puritans' may have influenced the council, but it is just as likely that the stained glass, copes and vestments were sacrificed as a demonstration of Stratford's loyalty to the Crown.

During this time John Shakespeare remained an alderman, and one

Archery practice

of Stratford's most prominent citizens. It was not long before he was given new responsibilities. In 1571 he was appointed High Alderman, which meant that he again exercised the powers of a justice of the peace, and also acted as the bailiff's deputy. The bailiff himself was Adrian Quiney, the High Street mercer, whom John had known for years; almost twenty years before they had been fined twelve pence each as jointly responsible for the dunghill in Henley Street. Quiney was an even more firmly established figure in Stratford than Shakespeare, having been bailiff as long before as 1559.

Early in 1572 the two men went off to London on council business (they received £8 for expenses). While they negotiated with the Earl of Warwick, John Shakespeare took the opportunity to indulge his passion for litigation. At the Court of Common Pleas at Westminster he pursued a debt of £50 owed him by a Banbury glover, and was himself sued for £30 by Henry Higford, who had been steward of Stratford at the time John had been bailiff. Higford tried again in 1578, but, like so many unlucky litigants, never succeeded in getting his money back.

At this stage in his life John Shakespeare must have been very well satisfied with himself. He had been chosen for his town's highest positions and could expect to be bailiff again at some time in the future. His family was still growing—Anne was born in September 1571 and Richard in 1574. And the ease with which he could support them all is proved by his purchase of two more houses, somewhere in the town, in 1575. At about this time he decided to apply for formal recognition of his status: he asked the Heralds' College to grant him a coat of arms. Possession of this would make him beyond question a gentleman; and since he could support the necessary style of life, no difficulties were likely to be made by the heralds. It seemed that John had secured the future for himself and also for his children.

Shakespeares at school and church

By this time the Shakespeare boys would have been learning their letters and starting their school careers. William would have entered Stratford Grammar School about 1571, at seven years old, followed by Gilbert Shakespeare some two years later. We cannot be absolutely certain they went there, but it fits all the known facts: the school was free; the boys were sons of an alderman and would have had no difficulty in securing admission; and the plays later written by William show evidence that he had received the standard grammar school training.

Before they went they would have learned to read and write. There may have been a Stratford 'petty school' for this purpose ('petty' being an English version of the French *petit,* 'little') or the teaching may have been done by a friendly neighbour. The lessons would have been based on a hornbook, which consisted of a single sheet of paper attached to a flat piece of wood with a handle (roughly the shape of a table tennis bat). The 'book' was covered with a sheet of horn, a cheap, hardwearing substitute for glass that helped to preserve the precious printed sheet as it passed through generations of grubby hands. The sheet itself was printed in black-letters, a bold 'gothic' script full of flourishes. Its twenty lines set out the alphabet, some syllables, and two religious texts which served for practising reading and writing, and anyway needed to be got by heart: the *In nomine* ('in the name of the Father', etc.) and the Our Father. The handwriting learned by the Shakespeare boys would have been a cursive form of the 'gothic', straggling and particularly hard to read. Among the upper classes the new Italian hands—ancestors of our ordinary and italic styles—were becoming universal, but they had not yet reached provincial Stratford.

Some girls might be taught the ABC from the hornbook, but that was as far as their learning would go unless they were destined to become great ladies. There would certainly never be any question of a girl going to school with her brothers. Women were the weaker sex, intended to be under the authority of the male and to bend their energies to housework, needlework, cooking and child-rearing. This was the traditional view and, as far as the people of Stratford knew, described the way things had always been. Even in the beginning Eve had been created after Adam, and only because he was lonely in the Garden of Eden.

A school lesson

So it was the boys who went down the High Street to the Guild hall, and on in to the schoolroom upstairs. This big room with its rows of heavy desks seems to have been in a bad state of repair during the 1570s, and William and Gilbert probably had most of their lessons in the Guild Chapel next door. Their day began uncomfortably early, at six o'clock in summer and seven in winter, with prayers, and carried on till about five in the afternoon with breaks for breakfast and lunch. To us it seems an unreasonably long, hard, grind—a six-day week with two half-days off and school time devoted entirely to class work: there were no games periods or art and woodwork classes (let alone filmshows) to vary the routine of constant application, enforced by strict discipline and the ever-present threat of a birching.

The Elizabethan attitude towards children was quite different from ours. By and large, children were seen as small, ignorant, undisciplined versions of adults, who had to be drilled until they behaved decently and had learned as much as was needed for them to take their places in society. Life was short, and the sooner they did so the better. These considerations applied only to the upper and middle classes, of course. The children of the poor, most of whom never saw the inside of a schoolroom, had much more fun and freedom for a year or two (if they had enough to eat)—until they were old enough to do odd jobs or go out into the world as servants.

Although severe by our standards, good and dedicated teachers were quite common; there were even some daringly advanced thinkers who believed that beatings did little good and that schoolboys worked better if their tasks were made interesting. Stratford attracted some well-qualified men, for the salary was generous. The teacher was paid £20 a year and given the use of a house near the Guild hall. Out of this he had to pay an assistant master, called an usher, who was in charge of the lower school (boys in their first three years).

The most important masters in William's and Gilbert's time were Simon Hunt and Thomas Jenkins, both Oxford men. Hunt, appointed in 1571, was a Catholic who evidently found his position becoming unbearable: in 1575 he left Stratford for Douai in Flanders, where there was a famous Catholic college for English refugees. There he became a Jesuit and went on to become eminent at Rome itself. Jenkins, a fellow of St John's, Oxford, left his position as master at Warwick School to take over from Hunt at Stratford; he must have been the chief academic influence on William and Gilbert. He was succeeded in 1579 by yet another Oxford man, John Cottom. In 1582 Cottom's brother, a Catholic priest, was executed for his missionary activities in England, and shortly afterwards Cottom left Stratford. He later settled in Lancashire and stalwartly paid regular fines for refusing to attend church.

These cases give some idea of the uncertainties of the seventies and eighties. It was not exactly a crime to be a Catholic, though Catholic *priests* were executed as agents of a foreign power—the Pope. But Catholics were under the heaviest possible pressure, and were finding it harder and harder to compromise with the Elizabethan system. Soon there were simply no Catholics left in official or public positions, with the exception of a few great nobles and some gentlemen in heavily Catholic areas such as Lancashire.

Stratford's town councillors may or may not have cared about the schoolmasters' beliefs, but it was never good policy to lose favour with the government. So it must have been embarrassing to have employed two 'unreliable' masters within ten years: and no doubt it was a relief when a solid Protestant, Alexander Aspinall, settled in and showed every sign of staying. Aspinall—another Oxonian—taught at Stratford until his death in 1624. In the course of time he also married a widow who carried on a thriving wool business, a clever stroke that gave him the money to become one of Stratford's leading citizens in the 1590s. If the younger Shakespeare boys, Richard and Edmund, followed their brothers to the grammar school, Aspinall was their main teacher.

Grammar schools were so called for the obvious reason that they taught grammar—*Latin* grammar. There was no study of English as such. The 'classical' tongues, Greek and Latin, had a towering prestige that is hard to imagine now: most educated people believed that everything worth thinking had already been thought, and perfectly expressed, by the Greeks and Romans. Classical models existed for poetry and prose, philosophy, and the arts of argument and eloquence (rhetoric). Even classical history was felt to be as interesting and relevant as anything more recent, for history was valued for the moral lessons it was supposed to teach, not as a re-creation of the past. The only non-classical authority—though the supreme authority—was the Bible, part-Hebrew, part-Greek; and even this had been best known for centuries in the Latin version, the Vulgate.

Latin had been the language of culture in medieval Europe, and remained the basis of all education even in the sixteenth century; Greek, though revived during the Renaissance, was never as widely taught. The Latin grammar used in every school was the textbook by William Lily, the first headmaster of St Paul's School. It contained plenty of tags and phrases that could be memorized and trotted out

43

in conversation, immediately establishing your status as an educated person. As he mastered his Lily, the schoolboy would move on to standard Latin authors such as Virgil, Ovid, Horace, Terence, Sallust and Cicero. The only thing to be said against them was that they were pagans (though Virgil had been partly Christianized because he had supposedly prophesied the coming of Jesus). So the syllabus also usually contained a few Christian writers—mainly near-contemporary Italians who wrote Latin verse of epic length and dullness. Such were Mantuan and Marcellus Pallingenius, both now utterly forgotten. William and Gilbert Shakespeare left school too early to study the patriotic Latin poems of the English schoolmaster Christopher Ocland, but Richard and Edmund may have had to endure his insipid *Anglorum Praelia,* about the battles in English history, and the *Elizabetha,* eulogizing the Queen. Both were prescribed reading in schools from the 1580s.

Question-and-answer, chanting in chorus, endless repetition: it sounds unattractive, but it did train the memory. It imprinted quotable quotes, information, and elementary logical and rhetorical devices in a way that was the more important because printed books were still not so very common; you had to carry a good deal of your knowledge about with you. And endless translating and retranslating did make a boy fluent in Latin and practised in writing English—which was as close as most schools came to teaching the native tongue.

The emphasis on Latin was justified by (among other things) its practical value: it remained the language of the legal profession, the civil service, the universities, medicine, diplomacy and international relations. Most learned treatises were still written in Latin, though the tradition was being challenged by books like *The Schoolmaster,* written by Queen Elizabeth's teacher Roger Ascham, and by Sir Philip Sidney's *Defence of Poetry.* The flourishing of poetry and the drama in English was establishing a near-equality for the native tongue, but when Queen Elizabeth visited a town she was likely to be greeted in Latin (or even Greek): in fact the process was so slow that, two centuries later, Doctor Johnson could still assert that only works written in Latin could hope for immortality.

The true school of English, in Stratford and other places, was the church. The greatest of all changes brought about by the Protestant Reformation was to substitute English for Latin in the services. The dignified and splendid language of the Book of Common Prayer and the Bible became rooted in English speech, familiar even to the illiterate. The translation of the Bible known to the Shakespeares was not the famous Authorized Version, which was made in the next

The Sunday sermon

reign. It was the 'Bishops' Bible' issued in 1568 and used in all the churches. At home the Shakespeares may also have possessed a Geneva Bible, a version translated in the city which was the headquarters of the strict Calvinist sect. Naturally the Geneva Bible was favoured by the Puritans, but it was also more widely popular because of its helpful—if sharp and controversial—commentary.

All the great events of life took place or were commemorated in church: christenings, carried out in the medieval font of Holy Trinity; marriage; death, and burial in the churchyard. And there was no question of ignoring the church for the rest of the time: as we have seen, attendance was compulsory. The ritual of Morning and Evening prayer on Sundays and holy days (holidays) must have sunk deep; and the church insisted on more than just a passive attendance. From a very early age the 'children, apprentices and servants' (often one and the same thing) were compelled to attend church for instruction in the Catechism: this too was laid down by statute. On Sundays and holy days they were expected to show what they had learned by delivering perfectly memorized answers in public. Thus the basic elements of their religion were thoroughly known, and its formulations came easily to the lips. The question-and-answer form of catechism and school teaching was natural in a culture on which printing had not yet made its full impact: it was the method used for centuries in medieval schools and universities.

Adult communicants were supposed to know still more. They should have been able to say the Ten Commandments, the Creed and the Lord's Prayer. Most clergymen would have been too discreet to press questions on prominent citizens, but we can be sure that the poor were officiously kept up to the mark; social superiority was much insisted upon in the Elizabethan period. All depended on the zeal and ability of the vicar. Many were themselves poorly educated and just about able to get through their duties. But Stratford seems to have got hold of good men, probably because the salary was adequate (£20 a year, like the schoolmaster's) and the burgesses were willing to boost it still further with gifts if they approved of the incumbent.

The enthusiasm of the Stratford burgesses was typical of an age when churchgoing was as much a pleasure as a duty, entertainment as well as edification, an intellectual and emotional treat as well as necessary for man's salvation. This was particularly true if the vicar was capable of giving a good rousing sermon. To do so he had to be a learned man, with plenty of good quotations at his command and a sound training in the arts of eloquence. Henry Haycroft was such a man: a fellow of St John's, Cambridge, and respectably married (a

Children at play

certain guarantee against Catholic sympathies in a clergyman). He was vicar of Holy Trinity from 1569 to 1584. His successor, Richard Barton from Coventry, seems to have been a puritan; his sermons were even better than Haycroft's, and he was so popular in Stratford that even after he had moved on to a richer benefice he was invited back as a guest preacher. Under these conscientious shepherds the young Shakespeares were no doubt thoroughly catechized.

The religious life of Stratford as a whole was divided between the Church of the Holy Trinity and the Guild Chapel. The church, a fine, large building, had every advantage but one: it was rather far away from the town centre. The Guild Chapel, with its 'papist' associations, might have been swept away altogether had it not been so conveniently situated. The Chapel bell summoned the town council to meetings; inside the chapel, schoolboys' and councillors' prayers were said; and the building was also used for special sermons and emergency services in plague time.

The vicar had a house in the Guild precincts, near the schoolmaster's: an appropriate enough arrangement since both were agents of authority, teaching received doctrines in which there was no place for doubt and discussion. The master was often himself in orders, and a few years earlier, in 1565, William Smart had switched from teaching the classics in the schoolroom to teaching the Gospel in Church and Chapel, taking the place of John Bretchgirdle, the vicar who had just died.

William Shakespeare and his brothers grew up under the shadow of these twin authorities, and it is this that makes their childhood so different from a modern boy's. They too played games and got into trouble; but for much of the time they were under stern discipline, drilled into good behaviour, and expected to memorize astonishing quantities of information. Most striking of all to anyone used to twentieth century methods, education was a one-way process. There was no place for suggestions, ideas, discussion or debate (except perhaps as practice in presenting a case): a boy went to school and church to learn a fixed body of information and indisputable wisdom. And when he had learned some appropriate part of it, he either moved on to Oxford or Cambridge, or one of the inns of court, or else he went out into the world. John Shakespeare's children went out into the world, much better educated than he had been, though lacking the final polish so desirable for a (would-be) gentleman's sons. Perhaps they would have been given it if John's fortunes had not changed dramatically before even his eldest son had left school.

Hard times

Some time around 1576, John Shakespeare was confidently applying for a coat of arms. Then, apparently soon afterwards, he got into serious financial difficulties, had to sell some of his most valuable properties, and dropped all his cherished civic activities. The record is clear enough, though the cause of the catastrophe remains a mystery. The most plausible explanation is that John had neglected his trade in favour of municipal affairs. After all, he had quite a large family to bring up, but in the years when he was giving so much of his time to the council none of the boys were old enough to take his place in the workshop or on the market stall; and a man cannot efficiently sell gloves and settle other traders' arguments at the same time.

If this is the correct explanation, John Shakespeare's position may have been growing weaker for some years before 1576; we can suppose that he had been steadily losing customers to the other Stratford glovers, but had relied on his accumulated wealth to see him through, and on his popularity to win back the lost trade. He was probably forced to recognize the truth by some unlucky stroke of business that required him to find a painfully large lump sum, and enforced immediate economies.

All this is admittedly speculation, though it fits the documentary record well. Alderman Shakespeare had been assiduous in his attendances at council meetings; suddenly, from 1577, he stopped attending altogether — a terrible wrench for a man of his sort, and one that could only mean that he was unable to meet the expenses involved. The council was evidently sympathetic, for the next year it reduced the contribution he was supposed to pay towards equipping a muster of soldiers (in the event he failed to pay anything). He was also excused from paying towards poor relief, and seems never to have been fined for non-attendance at council meetings—a hefty 6s. 8d. a time.

Things evidently went from bad to worse, for John was soon trying to raise cash on his wife's inheritance. He leased one of Mary's properties at a low rent in return for an immediate cash payment; mortgaged another to his brother-in-law, Edmund Lambert, in return for a loan of £40; and sold Mary's share in the Arden's Snitterfield estate. By this time, of course, the application for a coat of arms had been quietly shelved.

Preparing a meal

In 1579 John's little daughter Anne died at only seven and a half years old. This was one of those blows that parents had to expect in the sixteenth century, though it is not clear that they found it any easier to bear. A different kind of shock was the discovery that Mary was pregnant again—six years after her last child. The prospect of supporting and caring for another Shakespeare from babyhood onwards cannot have been alluring for a middle-aged couple already finding it hard to make ends meet.

Edmund Shakespeare's birth was registered on 2 May 1580. Shortly before this happened, his father was in obscure difficulties with the law. He was fined £20 for not appearing in Queen's Bench to offer sureties to keep the peace, and another twenty as guarantor of a Nottingham hatmaker, John Audley, who had also failed to turn up. Just how John Shakespeare threatened the peace is not known, though it is possible he was beating up his creditors; two years later he was asking Queen's Bench for protection against threats of violence from four men. But if John's offence was not violence, it must have been some other common one, since a hundred and forty-odd men were given similar fines at the same time. Most likely it was a matter of failing to attend church regularly. Such a failure might indicate extreme puritan sympathies (or, though less likely here, Catholic leanings), but it might equally well have been the only way to avoid being dunned for debt. The church door was an obvious place at which to lay your hands on a debtor, and probably the only one when the debtor had given up attending council meetings. . . There is no record of his having paid the Queen's Bench fine.

Two years later, John's eldest son got a girl pregnant and had to marry her. There was nothing unusual about this event, though John must have cursed William's poor timing, which brought one—and soon two—new dependants to the house in Henley Street. The girl was the daughter of one of John Shakespeare's aquaintances, Richard Hathaway, who had occupied a substantial farmhouse at Shottery, a village a few kilometres west of Stratford. Richard had died shortly before, and his daughter Anne may have been living at Temple Grafton when William Shakespeare came calling; at any rate it was there that they were married, conveniently far from wagging tongues at Stratford.

William may or may not have loved Anne Hathaway; she was too respectable to leave in the lurch, whatever his feelings, so there is no way of knowing what they were. At eighteen William was still very young to marry, especially since he had a way to make in the world; whereas Anne, at twenty-six, was past the normal age for a first marriage, and strikingly older than her boy husband.

John Shakespeare's first grandchild, Susanna, was born in May 1583, six months after the marriage of William and Anne. Two years later Anne had twins—Hamnet and Judith, named after the Sadlers, a baker and his wife who had a shop in the High Street. The arrival of two children in one year must have been another unpleasant shock for the impoverished household, and the fact that there were no more children after these, suggests that William removed himself from trouble and temptation by leaving Henley Street. After all, at twenty-one he was already the father of three children! Possibly he went first to an attorney's office or did some teaching; and by about 1588 he had gone off to London to seek his fortune.

Meanwhile John Shakespeare's civic career received its inevitable death-blow. In 1586 the council ruled that he must be deprived of his aldermanic office, for 'Mr Shaxpere doth not come to the halls when they be warned, nor hath done of long time'. In spite of which John continued to become involved in legal and financial tangles—which suggests that he was the kind of incurable optimist who cannot cope realistically with protracted difficulties. He could not pay his council dues and yet was ready to act as guarantor of other people's borrowings or good behaviour. In the very year of his expulsion from the council he stood surety for a tinker indicted for felony; in 1587 he was sued for part of a debt owed by his brother Henry, which he had rashly guaranteed; and in 1588 he began a long and complicated suit against his brother-in-law's son, John Lambert, in an attempt to either recover Mary Arden's property (forfeited because John had failed to repay the £40 borrowed) or squeeze another payment out of Lambert.

Four years later, in 1592, things were still no better. John Shakespeare's name is found on a list of people who had failed to attend church at least once a month, 'It is said . . . for fear of process for debt', notes the official record.

Gentlemen at last

Suddenly John Shakespeare went up in the world again, even higher than before. This was almost certainly not his own doing, but his son William's—a fact all the more surprising in view of William's dubious choice of profession.

For, some time in the later 1580s, William had decided to become a player—a member of one of the companies of actors that often turned up at Stratford to give a few performances. The players were rather like prostitutes, popular but disreputable. They were near-vagabonds who stayed out of trouble by taking the name and wearing the livery of some great lord. The Earls of Leicester, Warwick, Worcester and Essex, Lord Berkeley and Lord Strange—these and other magnates had their own 'Men', whom in fact they employed for only a few weeks in a year. For the rest of the time the players lived by performing in the few London playhouses (the only professional theatres in England, established since 1576), or by touring the provinces.

Stratford received all the noblemen's companies just mentioned; some of them, like Lord Berkeley's Men and the Earl of Worcester's Men, came three or four times in the 1570s and '80s. When a company arrived it gave a first, 'official' performance before the council in the Guild hall; so in the days of his prosperity John Shakespeare was quite familiar with plays. The average payment for these performances was about fifteen shillings, plus whatever could be collected by passing round the hat. Then there would be other performances in the courtyards of the Bridge Street inns, perhaps at the London rate of admission, a penny per person.

None of this would have pleased the puritans of Stratford. Puritans tended to condemn any form of entertainment as a distraction from work and godliness, but there were more specific objections to plays and players. Performances in inn yards encouraged tippling, swearing and rowdiness—undesirable at all times, but particularly so among the lower orders. The players themselves set a bad example, capering about and cracking a lot of dirty jokes—probably ad-libbing more freely (and dirtily) when the council wasn't there.

Some puritans condemned plays on even more basic grounds: they were impostures, lies: the players pretended to be lovers or kings or even *women* (played by boys), saying things they didn't believe and doing things they knew to be untrue. It was a naïve view, but hard to refute in the only terms people accepted—moral terms. To puritans it would have seemed ridiculous to suggest that drama might display moral insight, let alone amount to 'great art'. And the majority of people who enjoyed plays would have agreed with them. A few London sophisticates realized that drama of quality was being written by a new generation of university men like Peele and Marlowe, but everybody else continued to think of players as happy-go-lucky rascals.

If John Shakespeare had continued to be a prosperous burgess in the 1570s, he would have expected William to follow him into the gloving trade or some other solid line of business—so John's misfortunes may well have been decisive in making his son a great playwright. William no doubt joined one of the companies while they were at Stratford—perhaps in 1587, when no less than five visited the town. One of these, the Queen's Men, were certainly a man short at the time, for at Thame in Oxfordshire two of the players had fallen out and fought with swords; one, William Knell, had been killed by a blow in the throat. The Queen's Men were the finest group of performers in the country, since the Queen had formed the company by simply selecting the best actors from other companies, who were hardly in a position to resist the royal will.

William Shakespeare's next few years in London are of no concern here: all that matters is that he made a good deal of money, and made it fairly quickly. By 1596 John Shakespeare's application for a coat of arms had been renewed, probably at the instance of his son, now a successful poet-dramatist-actor-businessman. In October the application was granted. The grounds for doing so were that John's grandfather had served Henry VII and been advanced and rewarded by him; and that John himself had married Mary, one of the heirs of 'Robert Arden of Wilmcote in the said county, esquire'. Neither reason was very convincing: the grandfather seems to have been a fiction, and we have seen that Mary was only the eighth daughter of a very minor branch of the great Arden family. The truth was that in England gentility was mainly a matter of having money and possessions: when the heralds were satisfied that they were dealing with a man of substance, they happily found the necessary reasons for conferring a coat of arms.

A gross example of this occurred a few years later, when the question arose of adding the Arden arms to the Shakespeares'. Sir William Dethick, Garter King of Arms, calmly elaborated the Henry VII story by stating that the king had rewarded John's *great*-grandfather with lands and tenements in Warwickshire. The

Players performing in an inn yard

John Shakespeare's coat of arms

change of generation and fictional detail are typical of the surviving documents, filled with slips and contradictions. The whole procedure was a formality, but one that had to be approached seriously, even solemnly, by both applicants and heralds. Then all would be well provided the applicant did not claim to be related to any surviving family of distinction (those that had died out were fair game), and provided he was not caught up in the frequent and fierce quarrels between the heralds. This happened in 1602, when York Herald attacked Garter King of Arms for granting the Shakespeares a coat of arms that plagiarized those of a certain Lord Mauley. Dethick defended himself vigorously, pointing out that there were important differences between the two sets of arms. Significantly enough, he ignored the Henry VII episode and justified his grant of arms on the grounds that John had been a magistrate and justice of the peace, had 'married a daughter and heir of Arden, and was of good substance and habilite' [ability].

And so the Shakespeares became gentlefolk like their neighbours the Quineys, whose coat of arms probably suggested some features of the new one. The surviving draft of the Grant of Arms issued by the College of Heralds is an untidy document, covered in crossings-out and written in straggling old-fashioned handwriting with great loops, curves and flourishes. It is headed by the new motto of the Shakespeares, NON SANZ DROICT, 'Not Without Right'—a curiously defiant- or defensive-sounding assertion in the circumstances. And this is how the coat of arms is described in the gloriously strange language of heraldry, and with the original Elizabethan orthography:

> Gould [gold], on a bend sable, a speare of the first steeled argent [silver]. And for his creast or cognizaunce A faulcon, his wings displayed Argent standing on a wrethe of his coullers, supporting a speare gould steeled as aforesaid.

John Shakespeare was now entitled to display this design on his gates, on the front of his house, over the chimney-piece, on his tomb, and (if he so wished) on his plate and even about his person, on a seal-ring or some other ornament. And John's son William would have the double distinction of being not only a gentleman in his own right, but the son of a gentleman.

John's return to eminence came when the rest of Stratford had fallen on hard times, though John was probably too public-spirited to relish the reversal of fortunes. The town had recovered from the great flood in Armada year, when the Avon had burst its banks and swept away hay, carts and household goods, broken down both ends of Clopton bridge and unthatched the mill just beyond the church.

But the fires of 1595-6 had a disastrous effect on the town's prosperity. Fire was a permanent menace in any town of half-timbered houses, though the town council took such precautions as it could. All houses had to be provided with chimneys to carry the sparks away from the roofs; the corporation owned five hooks for pulling down buildings in the path of a fire so that it could be isolated; and the more substantial citizens kept one or two leather buckets outside their dwellings, ready for immediate use. In spite of all this, the fires destroyed much of Stratford, especially in the High Street area where houses were close-packed together. Shortages of corn added to the town's difficulties in the last years of the century, and in 1597 one of the members of the council, Adrian Quiney's son Richard, was sent to London to ask the Privy Council to let Stratford off its taxes.

From William's point of view too, there was an element of irony in the Shakespeares' new status. The family had become 'gentle'—thanks to him—just when his own hopes of a male heir had been destroyed: in August 1596, just before the Grant of Arms, Hamnet Shakespeare had died. William still had two daughters, Susanna and Judith; but however deeply loved, girls did not count in the same way. Right down to modern times men have set a high value on founding a 'dynasty'—a direct male line to carry on the family name, and perhaps some part of the 'founder's' personality. With no legitimate sons, and Anne around forty, this prospect had vanished for William.

All the same, he determined to show off his wealth in no uncertain fashion. His young manhood had been shabby-genteel, and it must have been a great source of satisfaction to be able to buy one of the finest houses in town. In 1597 William Shakespeare bought the imposing, five-gabled New Place, once the house of that William Bott whose bad temper had given John Shakespeare his chance of local distinction. The house was untouched by the great fires but was evidently in a state of dilapidation—which must be why Shakespeare got it at the bargain price of £60. Repairs began almost at once, and by 1598 Shakespeare was selling the left-over stone to the corporation.

Shakespeare's legal claim to the property was complicated by a sensational murder case. The previous owner of New Place, William Underhill, was poisoned by his eldest son, Fulke, shortly after the house had changed hands. Fulke was executed at Warwick in 1599, and the legal position remained obscure until 1602. Only in that year did the younger brother, Hercules Underhill, come of age and confirm the sale. Inevitably the confirmation cost Shakespeare a fee;

New Place under repair

but in those days it was wise to establish property rights as clearly as possible.

Presumably Anne Shakespeare and the two children had been living in Henley Street all these years, and now moved into New Place. William obviously spent some time in Stratford every year, but he must have spent longer in London with his company, the Lord Chamberlain's Men.

John, restored to fortune, started to go to law again. He made another protracted effort to get back the Wilmcote property from John Lambert, but without success. And he sued John Walford, of Marlborough in Wiltshire, to recover a thirty-year old debt: twenty-one pounds owing for twenty-one tods of wool which John had sold to Walford in 1568. (A tod was a load of 12-13 kilos.) One can only marvel at John's persistence and the slowness and uncertainties of the legal system.

On the other hand John made no attempt to rejoin the town council: after all, he must have been an old, old man by the standards of the time, well into his sixties. But the last we hear of him alive is, appropriately enough, in connection with the town's business. In 1601 alderman Richard Quiney made up a list of officials and reliable old Stratfordians who could testify to the rights of the borough, currently being threatened by a less sympathetic lord of the manor than the Earl of Warwick had been. John Shakespeare's name is on the list; and then, in September, it appears on another list—the register of burials in the Church of the Holy Trinity. It was the end of a career lived in obscurity and yet as dramatic and revealing in its way as any in the great world so far from Stratford.

Later Shakespeares

The main idea behind this book was to describe the Shakespeare family during a single lifetime, that of John Shakespeare. But it is worth having a rapid look at the family's later history, which gives us some interesting insights into the ups and downs of English life.

As master of New Place, William stocked up on corn and malt, became involved in a few legal wrangles, and steadily bought up land and tithes (originally the 'tenths' paid to the church; by Shakespeare's day just another form of investment yielding a regular income). He never became a member of the council, though he was involved in some civic affairs, notably a move to get a Bill through Parliament to improve the roads. At the same time he remained active in London as a shareholder in the Globe and Blackfriars Theatres, and as a playwright. Yet another irony of his life was that he could never now see one of his plays performed at Stratford, since a puritanical council had decided to bar the players for good.

Shakespeare's brothers were very unusual in one respect: they all remained unmarried. Some men did stay bachelors in Elizabethan England, but it was expected that most would marry; and for any but the highest class there cannot have been much sexual opportunity outside marriage or prostitutes—not, at least, once first youth was past. Lads and lassies might go a-maying and pair off while they did so; but a full-grown middle-class man was expected to behave more respectably—more *gravely*—than that. Perhaps, when John had fallen on hard times, the young Shakespeares were caught in the trap of shabby-gentility: being too good for common girls and not rich enough for respectable ones. But that is only a guess: we are never likely to know the truth.

The first of the brothers to die was the youngest, Edmund. Inspired by his brother's success, he had gone to London and become a player; but he gave up the ghost when he was only twenty-seven, in December 1601. A few months before, Edmund's 'base-born' (illegitimate) son had been buried at Cripplegate in the City of London. Edmund himself was buried outside the city limits, at Southwark on the South Bank, where the playhouses operated outside the control of the puritanical City fathers. Edmund's funeral, graced by the 'forenoon knell of the great bell', was expensive at twenty shillings, and may have been paid for by his brother William.

Mary Shakespeare, John's wife, died a few months later. Gilbert, only two years younger than William, followed in February 1612, aged forty-six. He was a haberdasher, and seems to have worked in both London and Stratford, where on one occasion he stood in for William to receive a deed to some land; the handwriting of his signature, more legible than his famous brother's, is that of an educated man. William's last surviving brother, Richard, died a year later at thirty-nine. Nothing at all is known about him.

By this time William himself had settled permanently in Stratford. His eldest daughter, Susanna, was already off his hands, having in

1607 married the physician John Hall, who built up a good practice and later became quite well known. Even at the beginning it was an excellent match for her, since Hall was a university man: he had an M.A. from Cambridge and had studied medicine in France.

The younger daughter, Judith, was less lucky. At thirty-one she was even older than her mother, Anne Hathaway, when she married; and though the groom, twenty-six-year-old Thomas Quiney, came from a good Stratford family (being the son of Richard and the grandson of Adrian Quiney), things seem to have gone badly from the first. Thomas and Judith were married during Lent, a close season for weddings, when a special licence was needed. (William Shakespeare had had to get one to wed his pregnant Anne during Advent.) They failed to do so, were twice summoned in vain to appear in front of the relevant ecclesiastical body, the Consistory Court, and so were excommunicated. Perhaps it was not as serious as it seems; at any rate it all blew over. But in the meantime an escapade from Thomas's past had caught up with him. He was compelled to publicly confess that he had had 'carnal intercourse'—sex relations—with one Margaret Wheeler, who bore his child; both mother and child died soon afterwards.

In spite of everything, Thomas and Judith set up shop in the Cage, on the corner of High Street and Bridge Street, selling wines and tobacco. Thomas became a town councillor and held several municipal offices, but evidently failed to prosper. He tried to sell the lease of the Cage, and in 1633 kinsmen took the property into trust for Thomas's wife and children. Business must have picked up later on, for Thomas kept on selling wine, though tradition has it that sometime after 1650 he deserted Judith and went to live on the charity of his brother, a wealthy London grocer.

If educated women were not uncommon among the nobility, they must have been almost non-existent among other classes. For even the daughters of William Shakespeare could not write. Susanna, though a fit wife for a highly educated man, could just sign her name. Judith could not manage even that: she just made her mark. Obviously William Shakespeare and his contemporaries thought that education was simply wasted on a woman.

Within two months of Judith's marriage, her father had died. Unlike John, buried in the churchyard, William Shakespeare was entombed in the chancel of the church itself. Later his widow (who survived him by nine years) had a bust of the poet put up in a niche on the wall above his grave. The bust was a standard, uninspired portrait job from a Southwark workshop, but adequate recognition of William's local standing—high, but not so high as that of the usurer

John Combe, who had lived at College Place, and whose tomb with recumbent effigy was a much grander affair, though also turned out at Gerard Johnson's workshop; and of course not in the same class as the Cloptons, who had a whole chapel of their own.

Unlike his father, the businesslike playwright left a will in which his goods were carefully disposed of. The most notorious provision was that his wife Anne should have 'my second-best bed with the furniture'—probably a practical afterthought rather than an insult; it added to the third of William's property to which the widow was automatically entitled. New Place was left to Susanna, and elaborate provisions were made for Susanna's and Judith's heirs.

The dying William had most of his trouble for nothing, for his line was not destined to survive even through his daughters. Susanna and John Hall had only one child, Elizabeth Hall, who married twice but had no children; she died in 1670. Judith and Thomas Quiney had three children: one was a few months old when he died; the other two died in the same year, 1639, aged eleven and nineteen.

Such facts—the dry record of heartbreak—bring home the hazardous nature of life in the Elizabethan age: you were lucky to survive childbirth, were vulnerable in childhood, and were likely to be carried off at any time in adult life. John Shakespeare's children lived to an average age of *thirty-five*, not counting the first Joan, who must have died as a child (so that the real average would be still lower). The average life-span of those who survived childhood was still only forty-eight; and it would have been lower but for the second Joan—Joan Hart.

This Joan lived to the ripe old age of seventy-seven, at Henley Street, to which William's will gave her a life tenancy. She was also the most fertile of John's children. By her husband, a Stratford hatter called William Hart, she had four children, who died aged four, ten, thirty-nine and (about) sixty-five. This last, Thomas Hart, was the ancestor of a family that has proved tenacious of life; it still exists—a present-day link with John Shakespeare and life at Stratford four centuries ago.